A SPECIAL BIBLE

For

_____

From

_____

_____

Date _____

"May the Lord bless you and keep you. May the Lord show you his kindness. May he have mercy on you. May the Lord watch over you and give you peace."

—NUMBERS 6:24–26 (ICB)

My Little Bible

Stories Retold by
Mary Hollingsworth

Illustrations by
Stephanie McFetridge Britt

WORD PUBLISHING
Dallas · London · Vancouver · Melbourne

MY LITTLE BIBLE ™

Stories retold by Mary Hollingsworth.
Managing Editor: Laura Minchew
Project Editor: Beverly Phillips

Scripture quotations identified ICB are from *The Interna-
tional Children's Bible, New Century Verison,* copyright
© 1986, 1988 Word Publishing, Dallas, TX.

Library of Congress Cataloging–in–Publication Data:

Britt, Stephanie.
   My little Bible / illustrated by Stephanie McFetridge Britt.
      p.   cm.
   Summary: An illustrated retelling of stories from the
      Old and New Testaments of the Bible.
   ISBN 0–8499–0824–8 (white)
        0–8499–1077–3 (pink)
        0–8499–1078–1 (blue)
   1. Bible stories, English.   2. Bible—Illustrations—
Juvenile literature.   [1. Bible stories.]   I. Title.
BS551 . 2 . B748   1991
220 . 9´505—dc20
                                            90–26726
                                            CIP
                                            AC

Manufactured in Mexico

96 97 98 99 00 DOR 24 23 22 21 20

Dear Reader:

The Bible is the most important book in the world.

Now you have your very own little Bible. It has 20 stories from the Old Testament and 22 stories from the New Testament.

The Old Testament tells how God made the world. It also tells about the first people. The New Testament tells about God's Son, Jesus, and how we can go to heaven.

It is good to read your Bible every day. It will help you stay close to God.

The Editor

Contents

New Testament Stories 51

OLD
TESTAMENT
STORIES

God Made the World

God made the world. And He made everything in it. He made the sun and moon. He made seas and dry land. He made plants. He made fish, birds, and animals. Then He made man and woman.

God was happy with what He had made.

GENESIS 1:1–25

Point to something that God made.

Adam and Eve

The man and woman God made were named Adam and Eve. They lived in a beautiful garden called Eden. They took care of the garden for God. The garden was full of wonderful fruit trees and plants. God let Adam name all the animals.

Adam and Eve were very happy in Eden.

GENESIS 1:26–2:25

Can you find the lion in the picture?

Noah's Big Boat

People on earth had become bad. Noah was the only good man. God decided to flood the earth with water. So, He told Noah to build a big boat to save his family. God sent two of each animal for Noah to put on the boat.

It rained for 40 days and nights. Water covered everything. But everyone on the big boat was safe and dry.

GENESIS 6:9–8:22

Where is Noah in the picture?

Joseph's Special Coat

Jacob had 12 sons, and Joseph was his favorite. Jacob gave Joseph a special coat. Then Joseph's brothers became angry. They sold Joseph to some men going to Egypt.

Joseph became a slave for one of the king's workers. And that's just where God wanted him to be.

GENESIS 37, 39:1–6

What colors are in Joseph's coat?

Baby Moses

When Moses was a baby, his mother had to hide him from the mean king of Egypt. She made a baby boat for him. She hid Moses in the boat in the Nile River.

The king's daughter found Moses and adopted him. Moses grew up in the king's own house, just as God had planned.

EXODUS 1:22–2:10

Who found baby Moses in the river?

A Burning Bush

When Moses was older he saw a burning bush. But the bush did not burn up. Moses went toward the bush, and God's voice spoke from the bush. "Moses, do not come closer. Take off your shoes. You are on holy ground."

Then God asked Moses to rescue His people from Egypt.

EXODUS 3:1-20

Why is Moses barefooted?

Leaving Egypt

Moses and his brother Aaron went to see the king of Egypt. They said, "God wants you to let His people leave Egypt." The king said, "No." So, God made ten terrible things happen to Egypt.

Finally, the king let God's people go. And Moses led them out of Egypt so they wouldn't be slaves.

EXODUS 7:10–12:33, 14:30–31

Can you point to the king of Egypt?

God's Ten Laws

After God's people left Egypt, God gave them ten laws. He wanted them to obey these laws. He wrote the laws on big stones and gave the stones to Moses.

These ten laws helped God's people to be pure and holy. The laws are called the Ten Commandments.

EXODUS 20:1–17, 24:12–14, 32:15–16

What is Moses holding?

Jericho's Walls Fall Down

God wanted the Israelites to capture the city of Jericho. Now, Jericho had big, tall walls around it. So, God had the people march around the city once a day for six days. On the seventh day, He had them go around seven times. Then He had them blow their horns and shout. And the walls of Jericho fell down.

The Israelites captured the city because they obeyed God.

JOSHUA 6:1–17, 20

When did the walls fall down?

26

Samson and Delilah

Samson was the strongest man who ever lived. What made him strong was a secret. Delilah was the woman Samson loved. She tricked him, and he told her his long hair was the secret.

Delilah had Samson's hair cut off while he slept. Then Samson was weak, and his enemies captured him.

JUDGES 16:4–22

Do you know a secret? Should you tell it?

Ruth and Naomi

Ruth married Naomi's son. But the son died. Then Ruth and Naomi moved to a country called Judah. Naomi's cousin Boaz lived there. He had a big wheat field. Boaz let Ruth pick up grain from his field to feed Naomi.

Boaz soon married Ruth. And they had a son named Obed. Naomi took care of Obed.

RUTH 1–4

Do you know any babies?

David and the Giant

David was a young, Israelite shepherd. Goliath was a big Philistine soldier. He was nine feet tall! Their countries were enemies.

One day David and Goliath had a fight. Goliath wore armor and had a big spear. David only had his slingshot and five stones. But God helped young David win the battle that day.

1 SAMUEL 17:4–50

Point to David's slingshot.

King David

God chose David to become king. All of God's people met at Hebron. There they made an agreement with David. Then the people poured oil on David's head to make him their king.

David was a great king. He ruled God's people for 40 years.

2 SAMUEL 5:1–12

Why was oil poured on David's head?

Solomon Is Wise

When David died, his son Solomon
became king. God said, "Solomon,
ask for anything you want. I will give
it to you." Solomon asked God for
wisdom to rule God's people well.
God was happy Solomon had asked
for wisdom instead of money. So, He
made Solomon the wisest and richest
man who has ever lived.

1 KINGS 3:4–15

Who is the wisest man God made?

Brave Queen Esther

Haman hated God's people, the Jews. He tricked King Xerxes into making a law to kill all the Jews. Esther was the queen, and King Xerxes loved her. But Esther was a Jew. She bravely told the king about Haman's trick. The king became angry and had Haman killed. Brave Esther had saved God's people.

ESTHER 2–9

Point to Esther's crown.

My Shepherd

The Lord is like a kind shepherd. And we are like His sheep. He gives us everything we need. He gives us a nice place to sleep, cool water to drink, and good food to eat. He protects us from our enemies. We don't need to be afraid because He is always with us. And we can live with Him forever.

PSALM 23

Who helps us when we are afraid?

Advice to Children

Do not forget what your father teaches you. Do what he tells you to do. If you do, you will live a long time. And you will be happy. Keep on loving and trusting your parents. Then God will be happy with you.

PROVERBS 3:1–4

Does obeying your parents make God happy?

Shadrach, Meshach, and Abednego

Shadrach, Meshach, and Abednego loved God. The king of Babylon built an idol for his people to worship. But these men would not worship the idol. So, the king put them in a hot fire. God sent His angel to save them from the fire. The king was amazed and began to worship God, too.

DANIEL 3:1–29

Who saved the men in the fire?

Daniel and the Lions

King Darius made a law for people not to pray to God. But Daniel kept praying to God three times a day. So, the king threw Daniel in a den of lions. God loved Daniel and kept the lions from hurting him. The king was surprised to find Daniel alive. Then King Darius believed in God, too.

DANIEL 6:1–23

Where is the lion?

Jonah and the Big Fish

God told Jonah to go to Nineveh to preach. But Jonah ran away on a boat. So, God sent a big storm. The men in the boat knew the storm was Jonah's fault. Jonah had not obeyed God. So, they threw Jonah into the sea. Then God sent a big fish to swallow Jonah. After three days, God made the fish spit Jonah onto dry land. Then Jonah went to Nineveh.

JONAH 1–3

How long was Jonah inside the fish?

NEW
TESTAMENT
STORIES

John Is Born

God's angel told Zechariah that his wife, Elizabeth, would have a baby. The angel told Zechariah to name the baby John. Zechariah didn't believe the angel. So God wouldn't let him talk until the baby was born. When the baby came, the people asked Zechariah to name him. He wrote, "His name is John." Then Zechariah could talk again.

LUKE 1:5–20, 57–66

What was the baby's name?

Jesus Is Born

An angel from God told Mary she would have a baby boy. The baby would be God's only Son. The angel told Mary to name the baby Jesus. He said the baby would grow up to save people from their sins. Later, the baby was born in a stable in Bethlehem. His bed was a box where animals are fed.

LUKE 1:26–33, 2:1–7

Where was Jesus born?

The Shepherds

The night Jesus was born, some shepherds were in the field with their sheep. Suddenly, they saw an angel. And they were afraid. The angel told them not to be afraid. He was bringing good news. He said Jesus the Savior had been born. The shepherds were happy. And they went to worship Jesus.

LUKE 2:8–20

What was the angel's good news?

The Wise Men

Some wise men from the East saw a bright new star. They knew the star was for God's Son. And they wanted to worship Him. So, they followed the star until they found baby Jesus. They gave baby Jesus some very special gifts.

MATTHEW 2:1–12

Point to the star.

The Boy Jesus

Jesus went to Jerusalem with His parents. He was 12 years old. After His parents had started home, they couldn't find Jesus. So, they went back to Jerusalem to look for Him. They looked for three days. Finally, they found Him in the temple talking to the teachers about God.

LUKE 2:41–52

Where did Jesus' parents find Him?

Jesus Feeds 5,000 People

More than 5,000 people followed Jesus far from town. Jesus taught them and healed the sick. In the afternoon, Jesus' followers wanted to send the people away to find food. But Jesus told them to feed the people themselves. The followers only had five small loaves of bread and two fish.

So, Jesus took the food, thanked God for it, and fed all 5,000 people.

MATTHEW 14:13–21

What did Jesus feed the people?

Jesus Stops a Storm

Jesus and His followers were in a boat during a bad storm. Jesus was asleep, and His followers were very scared. They thought Jesus didn't care if they drowned. So, they woke Him up.

Jesus told the storm to be quiet. Then the wind stopped, and the lake became calm. And the followers were amazed at His power!

MARK 4:35–41

Are you ever afraid during a storm?

Jesus and the Children

People brought their children to see Jesus. His followers tried to send the children away. But Jesus told them to let the children come to Him. He told His followers to love God like the little children do.

Then Jesus took the children in his arms and blessed them.

MARK 10:13–16

Do you think Jesus loves children?

Jesus and the Blind Man

Bartimaeus was blind. He was sitting beside the road. Then he heard Jesus coming. He called out for Jesus to help him. Jesus said, "Bartimaeus what do you want me to do?" Bartimaeus said he wanted to see again. Jesus healed Bartimaeus so he could see. Then Bartimaeus followed Jesus.

MARK 10:46–52

What would it be like to be blind?

The Wasteful Son

Once the younger of two brothers took his part of their father's money. He went to a faraway country. There he spent all his money. He was poor. He had no food to eat. He took a job feeding pigs. Then he decided to go home. He was sorry for acting so badly.

His father was so happy his son had come home, he gave a party.

LUKE 15:11–32

It is not good to run away from home.

Zaccheus Meets Jesus

Zaccheus cheated people by making them pay too much tax. One day Jesus came to town. Zaccheus was too short to see over the people. So, he climbed into a tree to see Jesus. Jesus saw him and told him to come down. Then Jesus went home with Zaccheus for dinner. And Zaccheus never cheated people again.

LUKE 19:1–10

How was Zaccheus able to see Jesus?

Lazarus Lives Again!

Jesus' friend Lazarus died. So, Jesus went to where Lazarus was buried. And Jesus cried. Then Jesus did a wonderful thing! He called out to Lazarus in his grave. He said, "Lazarus, come out!"

Then Lazarus came walking out of the grave. He was alive again! Jesus had raised him from death.

JOHN 11:1–44

Was Jesus sad when his friend died?

Jesus' Last Supper

The last supper Jesus shared with His followers was called Passover. He held some bread. He said the bread was like His body. Then He held a cup of wine. He said the wine was like His blood. He asked them to remember Him with wine and bread until He comes back.

LUKE 22:14–20

Does Jesus want us to remember Him?

Good News

God's Son, Jesus, was killed on a cross by His enemies. It was a dark, sad day. Jesus' friends took Him down from the cross. They wrapped Him in special cloths and buried Him. But three days later Jesus came back to life!

Jesus is more powerful than death. That is why Jesus can save us from our sins. And that is good news!

JOHN 19:16–20:18

What is the good news?

Jesus Goes
Back to Heaven

Jesus' work on earth was done. He told His followers to tell the whole world the good news about Him. Then Jesus disappeared into a cloud. He went back to heaven.

His followers were still looking into the sky when two men appeared. They told Jesus' followers that Jesus would come back to earth some day.

ACTS 1:6–11

Where is Jesus now?

Jesus' Followers Share

Jesus' followers shared everything they had. Each person had what he needed to live. The followers gave money, food, and clothes to those who needed it. And God blessed all the followers very much.

ACTS 4:32–35

What can you share?

Saul Meets Jesus

Saul was going to Damascus to hurt Jesus' followers. On the way, a bright light blinded Saul. Then Jesus' voice said, "Saul, I am Jesus. Go to Damascus and wait. Someone will come to tell you what you must do." Three days later, Ananias taught Saul to follow Jesus.

ACTS 9:1–19

What did Jesus tell Saul?

Peter and the Angel

Peter was in jail. He was sleeping between two soldiers. They had chains on Peter. Soldiers guarded the jail door, too. Suddenly, an angel came. Peter's chains fell off. And the angel led Peter out of the jail. Peter escaped! God saved Peter from his enemies.

ACTS 12:6–10

Who helped Peter escape from jail?

Love Other People

The best thing in the world is love. People who love others are kind and patient. They are not rude or mean. They don't brag about themselves. People who love are not jealous of each other. They don't get angry easily. And they are always there when you need them. They are nice to other people.

1 CORINTHIANS 13

How do you show love?

Obey Your Parents

Children, you should obey your parents the way God wants you to do. This is the right thing to do. God's command says, "Honor your father and your mother." If you do that, God promises you a long, happy life on the earth.

EPHESIANS 6:1–3

Why should you obey your parents?

Help Others

God wants us to help other people. We should love each other. We should welcome people to our homes. And we should visit people who are in jail. We should show them we care about them.

HEBREWS 13:1–3

How can you help others?

Jesus Will Come Back!

Someday Jesus will come back from heaven. He said, "I am coming soon!" When He comes, He will bring rewards with Him. He will give gifts to those who do good.

Those who believe in Jesus will go to heaven with Him.

REVELATION 22:12–14, 20–21

Will you be glad to see Jesus?